LIVING IN THE POWER OF PENTECOST

Living in the Power of Pentecost

Bishop Joseph C. McKinney

SERVANT BOOKS
Ann Arbor, Michigan

Copyright © 1986 by Joseph C. McKinney
All rights reserved.

Cover design and photograph by Michael Andaloro

Published by Servant Books
P.O. Box 8617
Ann Arbor, Michigan 48107

Printed in the United States of America
ISBN 0-89283-311-4

86 87 88 89 90 10 9 8 7 6 5 4 3 2 1

Contents

Foreword / 7

1. The Burning Question / 11
2. Praying the Scriptures / 23
3. Listening Prayer / 37
4. Keep Pentecost Alive! / 49
5. The Paraclete of Jesus / 63
6. The Face of the Holy Spirit / 79
7. Healed to Heal / 91
8. Jesus, Be Great in Me / 103

FOREWORD

Shepherd of Renewal

JESUS CHRIST IS LORD!

For the past seventeen years that simple yet profound truth has been the motto and the guiding principle behind the ministry of Joseph C. McKinney, auxiliary bishop of the Diocese of Grand Rapids, Michigan. He begins every sermon, every public address, every letter, and most phone conversations with the refrain, "Jesus Christ is Lord!"

It is unusual for a Catholic bishop to be so blunt about his relationship with Jesus Christ. But Bishop McKinney is an unusual bishop. He has come to be regarded as the "charismatic renewal's bishop" because he has been intimately connected with the movement's leaders since 1970. He has also been involved in Cursillo, Renew, and other programs of renewal for Catholic people, and his involvement has always been punctuated by a desire to relate as personally as possible with the ordinary lay people.

I'll never forget the time that Bishop McKinney invited me on a fishing weekend at his cabin in Michigan's northern woods. I had interviewed him for a magazine article and he wanted to get to know me better. What better way, he thought, than going after some bass? After an afternoon of fishing, the bishop discovered that I needed to learn how to filet a fish properly—the method I had taught myself as a boy was messy and wasteful compared to his smooth, neat, fileting style.

Night had fallen by the time we got around to the lesson. The bishop was interested not only in instructing me about cleaning the fish but also in learning my opinion about a divisive controversy that had recently erupted in the charismatic renewal. The scene that night is forever etched in my memory:

Bishop McKinney was standing at the cabin's main sink, clothed only in a pair of shorts soiled with fish blood, deftly slicing into the flesh of several large-mouth bass. (I am pleased to say that I caught those fish.) I was standing nearby, watching, truly amazed by his skill, trying to remember what my opinion was about the matter he was concerned with. After I had much less skillfully cleaned a couple of the fish, we put the meat on ice, cleaned up, and continued our conversation in comfortable chairs by a wood fire. I was fast asleep in minutes. I don't think he received any wisdom from me about the controversy in question, but I discovered what a fine man God has given to the people of western Michigan and the charismatic renewal.

A few months later I saw him again, dressed this time in liturgical vestments, celebrating mass for some ten thousand people assembled at the University of Notre Dame's Athletic and Convocation Center during a national charismatic renewal conference.

"Jesus Christ is Lord," he proclaimed at the beginning of his homily.

"Amen," "alleluia," the reply thundered from the assembled worshipers, men and women eager to hear from "their bishop."

Two sides of the same man: a friend and a pastor. That's the way I know him, and that's the way hundreds, maybe thousands, know him. Bishop McKinney is a good shepherd and a good man. God has given him wisdom through his many experiences with spiritual renewal in the church. That's what this book is about. There is a lot of practical wisdom in this book. The bishop takes an area like prayer or Bible study or liturgy and gives some simple, wise advice about how we can experience more of God's grace by opening our hearts wider to Jesus Christ the Lord. His advice often comes in the form of a clever slogan that you can memorize and use as a guiding principle in your prayer life.

As you read this book, try to see Bishop McKinney sitting by a fireplace giving you a personal teaching. That's the kind of man he is. If it were possible for him to sit in your living room and teach you, he would do it. Hopefully, this book will be the next best thing.

—Fred Lilly

ONE

The Burning Question

"BISHOPS, WHAT IS THE THEME of the church? You tell me what it is, and I will package it for you."

I can still hear the words of that question ringing in my ears. They were words that contained a seed, a seed that took root in my heart and grew up to produce much fruit in my life and my ministry as a Catholic bishop.

"What is the theme of the church?"

The question was addressed to a group of twenty-six Catholic bishops. We were meeting with media experts, exploring how we might communicate the gospel more effectively in the late twentieth century. The man who asked the question was troubled. He was a successful Madison Avenue public relations man. He was very good at the advertising business, but he knew that his effectiveness as a father to his teen-aged sons was waning. He was disturbed because his children were hearing a confused message from the pulpit. He did not know what to do about it.

This was the year 1970. The early 70s was a time of much confusion among Catholics in general. The man was pleading with us to give him something that he could hold on to—a sure message in a time of confusion. He was also trying to stimulate the group of bishops present at the workshop he was presenting to think about what we wanted to communicate to the world.

He convinced me that communicating a theme is the basic way to promote any product—even to spread the church's message of salvation in the person of Jesus Christ.

"What is the theme of the church?" That became for me the burning question. Does the church have a theme? Can we isolate one part of the church's multi-faceted message and call it a theme? The church teaches many things and stands for many things; to ask the question using modern management terminology: what is the bottom line? Is there one thing that is so basic that everything else we teach is built upon it? I left the workshop and began thinking about the question. What is the theme of the church? To my surprise, I had no immediate answer. It took a full eight months to discover the answer, and it was the Lord himself who had to show that answer to me.

During those eight months an advertising man's

The Burning Question / 13

simple question became a bishop's burning question. I knew that the answer had to be centered in Jesus because he is the head of the church. I had had a profound personal experience of this truth when I participated in the Cursillo movement, a movement of spiritual renewal and education within the church.

Although I knew that the answer to my burning question had to be related to Jesus Christ, I began my search in the wrong place—my own intellect. I had developed a habit of daily prayer, and so I reflected on the question often as I prayed. I also drove in my car a great deal—a bishop in a rural diocese like Grand Rapids, Michigan, spends a lot of time in his car. I thought a lot about the question as I drove to various places. My problem was not a lack of candidates for the theme of the church. I came up with a number of potential themes. But each one satisfied for only a short time, and then the mental search resumed.

"Jesus is a giver."
"Jesus is my brother."
"Jesus is the alpha and the omega."
"Jesus is the vine."
"Jesus is the redeemer."

Each one of these phrases came into my mind and was discarded. It's not that they aren't true. Each one revealed something to me about the character of the Son of God. But none of them held up as the theme upon which everything else depends.

During the months that I pondered the burning question, I was experiencing many new things in my life. Those were days of great experimentation in the church, and my life was filled with constant discovery of new ways of worship, new theological expressions, and new avenues of ministry for myself and for other Catholics.

One area where I experienced particular theological growth was in the sermons I delivered at confirmation services. I centered my sermons on the fact that Jesus is the one who comes among us in the name of the eternal God. I told those being confirmed that they were receiving the Holy Spirit in this sacrament to enable them to know Jesus more clearly and thus be able to center their lives in him, to become ministers of his gospel during their lives. Christians are the living pages of the book that Jesus wrote, I told them.

Everywhere that I preached this message I was told how people's lives were changed after they heard it. God had truly inspired my words and was working through them. Yet, I was still unable to find that one "theme of the church" that would tie it all together. The burning question did not go away, and the answers I was coming up with did not prove to be adequate.

As spring gave way to summer that year I began to look forward to a theological symposium for bishops that was to be held in July. The symposium was to bring together some fifty bishops who were to discuss christology—the area of theology devoted to exploring the meaning of Jesus Christ for human beings. Surely, I thought, I will find the answer to the burning question at this symposium. Some of the finest theologians in the church will be there. They will help me find the answer. I was very surprised, however, to find that rather than presenting answers to my questions, the theologians were presenting additional questions.

"We don't have the answers," they told us. "But we can help you examine the questions." The questions they posed were also surprising. Was the resurrection of Jesus a physical event or just a spiritual understanding on the part of the apostles? Do the Gospel accounts of Jesus' birth reflect reality? Was Jesus born with an understanding of his nature and his mission, or did he grow in this awareness as he matured? One theologian would present a talk that seemed to set us on a course that might dispel some of this confusion. But the next speaker would tell us to discard everything we had heard and then he would take us in a completely new direction.

That symposium prompted me to realize how much confusion there really was in the church. How desperately we need to find the theme of the church, I thought. But I did not find an answer to the burning question from the symposium. At one point

16 / *Living in the Power of Pentecost*

I turned to the Lord in prayer. "Jesus," I said, "you are supposed to be the answer. But you've become the problem."

I returned to Grand Rapids and continued with my busy schedule of confirmations in my own diocese and in a neighboring diocese. The more I preached at confirmations, the more convinced I was of the need to discover the church's theme. Yet, it continued to elude me. I questioned the Lord more closely. Why was this question burning in my heart? I didn't know anyone else who saw this as a great need. The more I questioned the Lord, the more I became convinced of my need and that of all the church to discover its theme. Clarity of vision and mission demanded that we isolate our theme and permit it to guide our pastoral practices, our theology, and our ministry.

So far I had searched for an answer to the burning question by examining theology, my life experience, and the experience of the contemporary church. However, I was unable to find it. The answer was not to be found in those areas. But I did find it—in prayer.

Later that year a group of thirteen priests met together for a retreat. We gathered at a beautiful spot—a cottage which several priests and I own jointly. The cottage is nestled in the midst of the Manistee National Forest in the woods of northern Michigan. It is a quiet, beautiful place—perfect for the kind of retreat we had planned. It was to be a time of prayer. Instead of listening to talks and reflecting on them, we decided to pray together and reflect on what we heard God saying to us.

The retreat leader was Father George Kosicki, the brother of a close friend of mine. Father Kosicki had been working with a group of young people in Ann Arbor, Michigan, who had been touched in a special way by the Holy Spirit through what was then called the Pentecostal movement. Father George's format for the retreat was to give us approximately twenty minutes of instruction about a form of prayer, and then we were to try that form of prayer for ourselves.

I had always wanted to be a man of prayer, but I felt as if I had not really learned how to pray. As the retreat progressed I discovered that I could grow as a man of prayer. It was a wonderful discovery. On the final day of the retreat Father George gave a talk on the topic "Jesus Christ is Lord." It was the most interesting talk I had ever heard. There was conviction and spiritual power in Father George's words. As I listened to that talk the Lord showed me the answer to the burning question, and as he did so he changed my life.

Here's what happened: Father George shared about how, after he came in contact with the young Catholic Pentecostals in Ann Arbor, he had studied the Scriptures for himself. As he did so he became convinced that the theme of the Scriptures—particularly the New Testament—is that Jesus Christ is Lord. He shared how this truth is the most ancient expression of Christian faith. It is found in many places in Scripture and in the writings of the early fathers of Christianity. The most ancient expression of the truth is found in the epistle to the Philippians: Let "every tongue proclaim to the glory of God the Father: Jesus Christ is Lord" (Phil 2:11).

Father George then explained what each of those words means for us, modern men, Christians and priests. As he did so I discovered why God had placed the burning question within my heart.

The name Jesus was given by the Father and means "the saving one." He is the one sent by the Father to save us. His whole life and ministry were aimed at the salvation of the human race. And he has continued to save us right down through the centuries. As a Catholic and a bishop I understood how, by his death and resurrection, Jesus saves us from sin and death. But during that talk I began to understand in more fullness what the word salvation means.

Salvation means "full health." It means that God wants us to have a healthy relationship with him, with our loved ones, and with our neighbors. It means that God wants us to have healthy bodies, minds, and spirits; he wants us to bloom as human beings and as witnesses for him. When we say that Jesus is the Savior, we mean a great deal more than being saved from hell.

The word Christ means "anointed one." Jesus was anointed with the Holy Spirit. We see this happening at his baptism in the Jordan (see Lk 3:21-22); we see the Spirit manifest as he preaches in the synagogue in Nazareth (see Lk 4:16-21); and we hear the promise of God given to us by John the Baptist and by Jesus himself: we will be baptized in the Holy Spirit by Jesus so that we can do the things that he does (see Mt 3:11; Lk 24:49).

It absolutely amazed me to see that Jesus, the focal person of my life, was so responsive to the Holy Spirit. It became clear that if the Holy Spirit played such an important role in the life of Jesus, I must also be responsive to the Holy Spirit. This is what turned my life around. As I heard about the many ways that people in our day were being responsive to the Holy Spirit, I was attracted to them.

Father George explained to us how Jesus is the "anointed anointer." He is anointed with the Spirit and he anoints us with the Spirit. The Spirit given us by Jesus enlightens us and empowers us. When we receive the Holy Spirit and respond to him, we no longer have to grope around in the dark. We have the certainty of our faith. The Spirit also empowers us to do the work God has given us to do. We receive the same power for kingdom building that Jesus received.

Jesus is also Lord. He is the one promised from ancient times as the messiah. The one looked forward to and longed for. The disciples acknowledged Jesus as Lord one day as he met with them on the shore of the sea of Galilee. When they discovered that he was the Lord of their lives, the one they looked to and obeyed, he was able to use them to be kingdom builders. The same is true for us today. When we acknowledge Jesus' lordship in our lives, when we dedicate our lives to him and decide to obey him alone, he can then use us in the task of kingdom building in our day.

Jesus is Lord of the universe. He is Lord of our lives. And he is Lord of the kingdom to which we belong—the community of the followers of God. I began that day to understand much more clearly how the church is a community of the followers of God: a people who through faith are called to hope, to love, to serve.

I also understood more deeply that the church plays a central role in helping me understand how Jesus Christ is Lord. Jesus shared his life with all who became his followers. But he shared his life in a special and central way with the church. I recalled then the challenge given to me as a seminarian studying for the priesthood. That challenge was to love the church. "Anyone can love an ideal church," I was told. "The question is, can you love the real church?"

When I decided to accept Jesus as my Lord, I also accepted more fully the challenge to love the church.

Love the church, wrinkles and all, was the image that came into my mind. That day I recommitted myself to building the kingdom of God with and through and in the church because there, above all, Jesus is Lord for all the ages.

The more I look at Jesus as Lord, the more I understand that there lies the power the church needs to overcome evil in the world, to build the kingdom of justice, love, and peace that is God's will for his human family. The incarnation continues as God takes flesh in our lives and calls us to union with Jesus.

So there I had it—the theme of the church. Jesus Christ is Lord! That simple phrase summed up so well everything I knew about the church. Everything I knew about Jesus being active in history among humans. Father George told us that he had arrived at this discovery while he was praying. When he discussed it with scripture scholars—men who had spent years of their lives studying Scripture—they told him that he had found the key to the good news.

Jesus Christ is Lord! That is the most ancient and most profound act of faith for Christians. It became my act of faith. At the end of the retreat, I fell on my knees and asked Jesus to become my Lord. I asked him to give me a new gift of prayer. I wanted to become a believer who prayed over the Scriptures so that God might make them a source of power for me.

I asked Father George to pray over me in the style of Pentecostals. The fruit of his prayer was that I began to see ever more fully how beautiful this truth is: Jesus Christ is Lord!

In fact, for more than seventeen years now I have started every homily, every talk I have given, with that expression. Jesus Christ is Lord. These words constitute our formula of faith, but they are much more than that. They are also the best summary of the message of the gospel, the word of God which must take root in our lives. The more the word of God takes root in our lives, the more Jesus becomes the focus and the dominant influence in our lives. Jesus is the word made flesh, and as the word takes flesh in us, we abide in him and he in us.

Jesus described his words as seeds. He said that if we open our hearts and minds to his words, they would take root and grow into beautiful, fruit-bearing trees of faith. The more we become like the Lord, the more fruitful our trees of faith become. This process can only happen if we are people who know and love the Scriptures. To know them we must learn not only how to read the Scriptures but also how to pray the Scriptures. And that is the subject of our next chapter.

TWO

Praying the Scriptures

I WAS IN AWE the first time I had the opportunity to enter the home of Joseph Cardinal Suenens. He is a famous man, a leader in the church, widely respected. The contribution that he made to the church during and since Vatican II is immense. Small wonder that a bishop from Michigan was humbled to be invited to the Cardinal's Palace in Brussels, Belgium.

He had invited me to discuss with him a book he had recently written. The book, *A New Pentecost?*, has become one of the most influential books among people interested in spiritual renewal within the church. I told him that I had read the book but that I had not yet had an opportunity to purchase a copy for myself. With that he left the room and returned a few moments later with a copy as a gift for me. He opened the front cover to write a personal message to me, but he suddenly stopped; he looked at me and said, "Let's pray for a scripture text."

I was surprised by this. It isn't the kind of thing I expected a man of his stature to say. We prayed for a few minutes and then the cardinal opened the Bible at random and placed his finger on a passage. He read the passage to me, then wrote it on the title page of the book he was giving me as a gift. The passage has come to be very meaningful for me:

> At that moment Jesus rejoiced in the Holy Spirit and said: "I offer you praise, O Father, Lord of heaven and earth, because what you have hidden from the learned and the clever you have revealed to the merest children." (Lk 10:21)

That text contains several phrases that have great meaning. The first is, "Jesus rejoiced in the Holy Spirit." Jesus manifested joy because of the action of the Holy Spirit in his life. As followers of Jesus we can also be joyful when the Holy Spirit is active in our lives.

The passage also speaks about the learned and clever missing what God reveals to the merest children. I believe that learning how to read the Scriptures as a child listening to the stories of a parent makes all the difference in the world. The Scriptures contain words of instruction and encouragement from a loving Father. When I approach the Bible in this way, it becomes alive for me, full of meaning. This is the approach I have learned to take in praying over the Scriptures.

Only once in my life have I had the experience that Cardinal Suenens had that day in his home. When I open the Scriptures at random, I generally do not find a passage full of meaning for the moment. But one time I did have that experience. I was in the midst of a search, which lasted for several months, for an answer to a problem. In desperation one day I cried out to the Lord for comfort and wisdom. "Lord," I prayed, "I've seen other people receive meaningful passages from you, but that never happens for me. I really need one now."

On that occasion the Lord gave me a passage that helped me and has since helped other people who have come to me with similar problems:

> Let us keep our eyes fixed on Jesus. . . . hence do not grow despondent or abandon the struggle. . . . Endure your trials as the discipline of God, who deals with you as sons. (Heb 12:2-7)

I read the passage and then put down my Bible to think about it. I recognized that God our Father had treated his beloved Son Jesus with a host of rejections in order that he might keep his eyes fixed on the will of his Father. Mary and the apostles had similar experiences. And so, I discovered, when I suffer rejection I can turn it to my advantage by using it as an opportunity to keep my eyes fixed on the Lord. The passage helped me recognize that there is something of a good coach in our heavenly Father. He does discipline us for the game of life because he wants us to be victors.

Although there was prayer involved in both of these instances, when I speak of praying over the Scriptures I have something else in mind. As I have prayed over the Scriptures during the past seventeen years, I have developed a system which allows God's word to act as a seed in my life. I do believe it is important to pray over the Scriptures.

Many people, when they decide to start reading the Bible, start with Genesis, chapter one and try to read through the entire Bible in sequence. I think it is much wiser to read smaller sections of Scripture day by day and pray over them. The method that I follow is this:

First, I choose a passage, sometimes several passages. Choosing them is no big problem. I may have run across one in my reading that I make note of for later reflection. Or I may have heard a reading at a liturgy that I want to reflect on further. Or I may decide to read a particular book of Scripture through section by section over the course of many days or even weeks.

Second, I take some time to relax, set aside distractions, and get my mind, my spirit, and my body lined up in the presence of God. I find that the most effective way to do this is to start by praising God. I will hum or sing a hymn, then I offer some spontaneous words of praise to the Lord.

The third step is to pray to the Holy Spirit, asking him to give me wisdom as I read and reflect on the passage I have chosen.

Next, I read the passage, paying special attention to its "now" meaning. What do these words say to me right now? To discover this I must go through several steps. The first step in discovering the "now" meaning of a passage is to know something about its "then" meaning. This comes through study. We need to turn to good Bible commentaries so that we can know what was the inspired thought in this passage. Some recently published Bibles have good footnotes that help with this. What is the religious truth that the author was trying to express when these words were recorded? The revelation that God is offering as my "now" spiritual food cannot be different from what he intended the original audience to understand.

Once I know something about the "then" meaning, I reflect prayerfully and with faith on the passage's "now" meaning for me. I find that prayer is vital if I am to successfully apply the Scripture to my own situation. God has a way, when we are silent in his presence, of bringing inspirations to light.

Inevitably I find an inspiration which brings the "then" meaning of the passage to a "now" meaning for me.

I can remember reading in chapter seven of Matthew's Gospel where Jesus contrasts the wisdom of the man who builds his house on rock with the foolishness of the man who builds his house on sand. When I read that, I understood that the Lord was saying to me that his words, his truths, are "rock" truths. The heavens and the earth will pass away, but his word will never pass away. That is the "then" meaning, the truth that Jesus was teaching on that occasion.

As I searched out the "now" meaning, it suddenly became clear to me that I was more like a bobber in the ocean—every wave that came along seemed to lift me and toss me in one direction or another. I was giving newspapers and books as much priority in my life as I was giving to the word of God. I was intrigued by every new theory that came along. God's word, I discovered, was not the foundation stone of my life. Whatever made sense to me was more important.

It became very clear that if I wanted my life to have a solid foundation I would have to give the Scriptures precedence over the other things I read. Any modern writings that do not submit to and build upon the truths of Scripture are now suspect in my mind. Coming to understand the "now" meaning of

Scripture is very important for those of us who want to live the Christian life.

Praying over the Scriptures has become an important part of my daily hour of prayer.

On one occasion I had the distinct privilege to be invited by scholars at the prestigious Biblicum in Rome to present a short conference to students earning advanced degrees in the Scriptures. I was asked to give the students my perspective on how they should teach about the sacred Scriptures once they returned to the United States to teach courses on Scripture in the seminaries. I remember very clearly praying to the Lord, asking him to inspire me. I was overwhelmed because it was clear that in the area of academic training all the students were way ahead of me. They were experts in ancient languages, anthropology, theology, and many other areas.

I did tell them how important it is that as scripture teachers they be men of faith and men of prayer. I have been immensely blessed by the work of scripture scholars who had obviously prayed and brought their faith to bear as they studied the word of God. I had also been terribly disillusioned by the work of scholars who studied the Scriptures from the point of view of pure science. I found that they tended to cast aside the possibility of revelation; they tried to tell me what the Scriptures did *not* say. I am much more interested in what the Scriptures *do* say than in what they don't say.

What is the authentic revelation in the Scriptures? That's the important question. We can discover this revelation only by praying over the Scriptures and approaching the written word with faith in our hearts and belief in our minds.

One of the good fortunes I have had as a priest is the opportunity to preach often about the Scriptures during the celebration of the Eucharist. The church exhorts her priests to preach about the Bible readings at every mass. I have found that this is the most rewarding part of my day. I have discovered the importance of the discipline of sitting in the presence of my God for an hour before each day's mass so that I can discern the "now" meaning of the scripture readings for that day's liturgy.

I like to follow the method that is employed by the Liturgy of the Hours (formerly called the Divine Office). This prayer form calls for vocal praise of the Lord. It calls for singing and praying the psalms. Then comes the moment when I invoke the Holy Spirit and pray over the readings that the church presents for the liturgy of the day.

I find that it is vital to my spiritual well-being that those words pass not only from my mind to my lips but also from my mind to my heart and thereby become integrated into my own life. Then I search for a way to express what I've learned to others when I preach the homily.

I like to preach about Bible stories like that of the little man Zaccheus. This man was open to the Lord's work in his life even though he was not a Jew. We don't know if he had any religious belief; perhaps he was a pagan. But he thought that Jesus had something to offer him, so he ran up ahead of the procession accompanying the Lord that day and he climbed into a tree. When Jesus came by, he stopped and told the little man that he would stay at his home. Zaccheus was so honored by this that he hurried home and made a great feast in honor of Jesus. He exposed his whole life to the Lord, and he grew as a man of generosity because he had experienced the generosity of Jesus.

It is one thing for us to look at Zaccheus and to admire him for the courage he showed by opening his life to Jesus. It is something else for us to be Zaccheus. Yet that is precisely how we should respond to the Scriptures. We should be so overwhelmed by the vision and the courage of Zaccheus, who accepted the Lord's invitation to change his life, that we do the same. When we read that passage, we should put down our Bible and turn to the Lord in prayer, asking him to come into the home of our hearts to change us. He will come if we ask, and he will make demands of us as he did of Zaccheus. Do we have the courage and the wisdom to obey the way the little man did?

Every time that I have the opportunity to receive

the Holy Eucharist, I have the opportunity to be Zaccheus. Jesus comes in the Eucharist as a guest in my heart. Am I overjoyed? Am I eager to commit my way of life to the Lord?

This is only one example of the good fruit that can come from praying over the Scriptures. This discipline blesses my life in so many ways.

One day as I was praying, God touched me very deeply. The gospel passage for the day was the baptism of Jesus in the waters of the Jordan by John the Baptist. That was a very welcome scene for me personally because I had learned from scripture scholars that this was the moment of transition between Jesus' private life and his public ministry. It was, therefore, an important moment for Jesus. Praying over that passage became an important moment for me. At the moment the skies open and the Spirit descends, it becomes clear to all that Jesus is uniquely anointed by God for ministry. God used that moment to dramatically announce Jesus as the representative of the Most High to the world of men and women.

In his account of this important event, Luke shows us what a key role the Holy Spirit played in the life of our Lord. The result of the baptism of Jesus is that he was filled with the Holy Spirit, led by the Holy Spirit, and he went out in the power of the Holy Spirit. Those theological insights deeply moved me, and I began to actively pursue a devotion to the Holy Spirit because I recognized that Jesus considered the Holy Spirit so important in his own life and ministry.

That day I approached my prayer over the Scriptures differently than usual. Because I had already contemplated this mystery many times and had experienced profound effects in my own life, I decided I would just sit back, relax, and relish the happy memories of the scene at the Jordan. As I did that I experienced something very profound: my prayer hour was relaxed; instead of actively contemplating the scriptural scene, I was swimming in the mystery and delighting in it. It was one of my most profound experiences of God's action during prayer.

I recall what happened very clearly. I felt challenged to enter into the skin of Jesus. This had never happened before. I had always inserted myself into a Bible story by imagining myself as another person contemplating Jesus. I had been Zaccheus, John the Baptist, a shepherd at Bethlehem, a Roman soldier at the foot of the cross, Peter running to the tomb. But never Jesus. That struck me as being presumptuous, perhaps a bit blasphemous. However, on this particular occasion God thought differently. He wanted me to envision myself as Jesus being baptized in the Jordan, receiving the Holy Spirit, being sent forth to minister in the power of the Holy Spirit. And what did I see?

I remembered that in Jesus God had taken on all of the characteristics of a human being except those that lead to sin. In the midst of that mystery, as I walked in the water with Jesus, I experienced the Lord moving in me, leading me, blessing me. Then the moment came when the heavens opened and the voice of the Father issued forth: "You are my beloved Son. On you my favor rests" (Lk 3:22).

I found myself suddenly transported in prayer. I saw the heavens open and God speaking loudly. What is he saying? Why these words? This was a rare moment in Scripture. God hardly ever spoke from the heavens this way. It was clear that the Father wanted there to be no doubt in the minds of anyone: Jesus is the beloved Son. Hear him and you hear the Father. I was amazed and moved by the clarity of God's intention: Jesus was to speak for him. Then I was moved to dialogue with Jesus.

What does it feel like, Jesus, to know that you are the beloved Son? What does it feel like to know that the Father is pleased with you? Those questions triggered a very deep time of prayer and contemplation of the mystery that defies words. It became totally clear to me that Jesus knew who he was and what his mission was. God the Father had no doubt about Jesus, and Jesus had no doubts about himself or his ministry. He was to represent God to the world. He was to make the decisive move of God in the history of salvation. His teaching and the giving of his life would change the world forever. And he knew it at that moment.

What did that mean for me? I believe that God wanted me to know that I too am a beloved son. He wanted me to know that if I put God's will first in my life, the Father would be well pleased with me also. He wanted me to know that I can receive the Holy Spirit and be empowered by him to engage in successful ministry in the kingdom of God.

I also experienced God telling me to relax, to remember that I cannot win his love or merit his blessings. He takes care of me because he loves me. Now, whenever I am discouraged or depressed, I recall that experience. I remember what God said and how he showed me his love. I am comforted when I remember that I am a beloved son of God and that nothing in this world can take that from me.

By learning how to pray over the Scriptures I have discovered the marvelous mystery that God wants to reveal his love and his word to me on a daily basis. God wants to live more fully in the life of every Christian. He wants us to be pages of the gospel. The good news is to live in us, and this happens as we pray over the Scriptures.

In 1985 I had another great privilege. I spent ten days at Immaculate Heart Retreat House in Spokane, Washington, immersing myself in the Scriptures under the direction of Monsignor David Rosage, one of the world's leading retreat masters.

Monsignor Rosage encouraged me to immerse myself in the Scriptures as if I were taking a sunbath in the presence of God. That image of a sunbath made those days a glorious time of experiencing the love of God for me.

The great American heresy is that if we work hard enough we can earn anything, even the love of God. The truth is that all we need to do is accept God's love, which is freely given, and allow it to transform us. I believe that the best way to allow that to happen is by praying over the Scriptures. God wants to transform the world through love, and it is only inasmuch as we can receive and radiate that love that that can happen.

When we pray the Lord's prayer we say, "Your kingdom come; your will be done on earth as it is in heaven." If God's name is not held in our hearts, if his kingdom is not within us, then his kingdom will not come into the world. As we pray through the Scriptures we receive his love into our lives and we place ourselves fully in his kingdom. Then we become his instruments for transforming the world. If we intend to transform the world, we must be very much in tune with God, and this involves learning how to listen to God. A truly skillful listener is the person best able to minister God's love to a world that stands so much in need of it. Let's now turn our attention to this important spiritual skill.

THREE

Listening Prayer

ONE AUTUMN MORNING I got up before dawn. It was October, deer-hunting season in Michigan. As I dressed and made my way out of the cabin into the still of the predawn darkness, I was filled with excitement. I bumped into a number of trees as I struggled to keep on the path through the woods that led to my favorite hunting spot. I would wait there, perhaps for many hours, hoping for deer to appear.

As I walked I began to wonder why I call this recreation. What is so special about this day? Why do I seem to be anticipating something unusual and exciting this morning?

I arrived at my destination before I answered that question. A deer hunter must be absolutely still because deer are very alert, cautious creatures. They will run away at the slightest hint of danger. So I sat there, trying also to be alert, to be ready for any movement that might signal the approach of a deer.

Suddenly an orange tint began to appear in the eastern sky. Soon the entire sky was filled with the subdued shades of orange and pink that announce the sunrise. Then the magic moment—the sun itself appeared, huge and orange, on the horizon. I don't remember the scientific explanation for it, but the sun appears to be about twice its size when it makes its first appearance each morning. Actually, I wasn't too interested in scientific explanations that morning. I was silently contemplating the majestic scene that greeted my eyes. There is nothing so beautiful as a sunrise on a cloudless morning.

As daylight began to take hold in the woods, I began to distinguish the various trees that were around me. The trees were as colorful as the sky because it was October and the fall color was at its height: I was surrounded by gold, red, orange, yellow, and green—a symphony of wondrous color. A gentle breeze stirred the leaves, and birds began to chirp in the trees, singing their songs to one another. God was touching the earth and the earth's life was responding in all its vigor, in all its beauty.

Suddenly I heard the rustle of leaves on the ground, but it wasn't a deer. Squirrels in search of winter food were running here and there. As I watched them the words of the psalmist came to me: "Be still, and know that I am God" (Ps 46:10).

That morning is etched in my memory because I discovered the beauty and power of my God in a new way. It was a profound moment. I had anticipated the movement of deer, but I discovered the glory of God. I try now to make it back to that spot each year in early October. Nowhere on earth is as beautiful because there I discovered God in the majesty of stillness and created life.

Stillness, openness, expectation. Those are very important ingredients in a healthy prayer life. Those are the ingredients that can make morning prayer truly significant. I try to spend that time in silence to dispose myself to what my God will say to me. Expectation is a key part of prayer.

One of my brother priests, my closest friend, and I often pray together in the stillness of the morning. Our routine is to pray quietly in the same room, then share with each other the insights that have come from that prayer time. Every time we pray together I benefit from it. But one time in particular stands out. On that day my brother told me about a visit he had recently had from an American Indian woman who was eager to know more about the "God of the Christians."

He talked with her on several occasions and, as he got to know what was in her heart, he was amazed by the sense of God's majesty and presence that she possessed. One day the woman's secret came out. Her mother, she said, taught her to value the dawn. Every morning she sat in stillness and watched the dawn. "This is where I find God," she said.

That statement is a profoundly valuable one regarding prayer. There are those moments when God comes before us in such majesty and glory that we cannot find the words to describe it. For me, those moments are wrapped in stillness and none is more profound than the beauty of the dawn. In moments of stillness, God's word will find its place in the heart of our being. Those are special moments of prayer: the moments that form us into the individuals that God wants us to be; the moments when we permit God to reach into our hearts and speak to us of life; the moments when we allow him to give us his wisdom and his insights into who we are and what we are about.

I have another close friend, my cousin. He is my confirmation sponsor and he is also a priest. I don't see him often because he lives a great distance away. But when we are able to get together, our visits are filled with great awe and wonder. I remember driving one time with him to visit some relatives. As we talked we discussed the goodness of God and the wonderful things that were happening as more and more people discovered the significance of the Holy Spirit in their lives.

My cousin is really in touch with many such people because he is an effective parish priest. He has always centered his spirituality in the Scriptures. That day he spoke a word that has continued to be a word of great wisdom for me.

"Do you know what a coincidence is?" he asked.

I knew he didn't want to hear me paraphrase Webster's dictionary, so I deferred.

"A coincidence is a minor miracle when God stays anonymous," he said.

I laughed at this, but I was thrilled in my spirit also. I recognized the great wisdom in that sentence. It reminded me of what was so true about the lives of the faith people of the old covenant—the Israelites, the people who developed the Scriptures under God's inspiration. An astute Israelite could see the hand of God in most events that happened around him. He could see God's hand delivering his people from the slavery of Egypt. He could see the hand of God again and again in the history of his people and in his own life. Many of these moments can be passed over as having natural, sociological, or historical explanations. But an Israelite would correctly see the hand of God because he had faith. His faith told him that this was not just a fortunate moment, not just a coincidence, but that the hand of God was in that moment.

The more one listens in prayer, the more one discovers the hand of God in the many details of daily life. Some of these are so subtle that we dare not tell them to people who want proof. These are "minor miracles," but they are indeed miracles because God is present, he is active, and he does care about even the small details of our lives.

When we learn to listen in prayer we "know with our knower" that God is present and acting. I don't know of any way to develop this sense except by developing a habit of regular quiet prayer.

It seems to me that the key to a successful, peaceful life is to learn how to rely on God. The picture of the bird making lazy circles in the sky has always taught me something about this. The bird has a sense for finding the air currents and riding on them. He only has to exert energy when he needs to adjust to a change in the current. All he has to do is to be alert to the wind's movement. He adapts to it and then he lets the wind do the work.

This is also the picture of the Christian. The movements of God in our lives can be compared to the wind which the bird rides—his presence surrounds us constantly. We need to place ourselves on the currents of that wind so that we can ride with it. As we develop this spiritual sense, life has new peace, new meaning, new joy. It is important that each day has its still moment when we can become aware of God's actions and begin to flow with them—it leads to majestic flight.

I used to believe that prayer consisted of making words. Conversation with God tended to be a one-way street. I talked to God in spontaneous prayer, I read the words of Scripture, and I prayed some of the ritual prayers I've memorized over the years. I was so busy that God rarely had a chance to enter into the conversation. It should be clear by now that I believe that spontaneous prayer, ritual prayers, and reading Scripture are very important. God uses each of these to stir up his Spirit in us, to give us insight and inspiration. Each of these forms of prayer is like a leg of a tripod—each leg is vital for the tripod to stand up correctly. But a balanced Christian life is more like a table with four legs. Such a life needs spontaneous prayer, liturgical and ritual prayer, scripture reading, and silence. If we are never silent, God never gets his turn to speak and our lives will therefore not become all that he wants them to be.

Fortunately, since I've surrendered my life to Jesus Christ who is my Lord, I've learned to give God that quiet time to speak to me. As I've learned the value of listening prayer, I've found the direction that I need to live each day and the power that I need to become a "page of the good news" helping to advance the kingdom of God in our day.

The Catholic church has always encouraged devotion to Mary, the mother of our Lord. The biblical image of Mary is very rich. As we explore the images of Mary revealed in God's word, we see why devotion to our spiritual mother is so important.

The image of Mary presented in the early chapters of the Gospel of Luke is one of Mary at prayer. Mary is overawed to find out that she is special to God. This is what we all find out as we stand before our God in silence—we discover that we too are beloved sons and daughters of God, that God wants to work wonders in our lives. God gives us each day as a time during which he can bring forth power and love into our lives.

The image of Mary in prayer before God synthesizes not only the individual before God in prayer but also the church in prayer. She is clearly showing us how we must have a stance of listening. And, as her life so clearly shows, listening must give way to obeying throughout one's life.

Another striking passage in the Bible is Jesus at prayer in the garden the night before he died for the salvation of all human beings. Jesus, like Mary, came before the Father to listen and to obey. In both instances it is the will of God that prevails. Jesus and Mary are listening to God, responding to his call. The key prayer in both examples is the "amen" prayer. They hear God and obey him.

When we come before our God we should also be ready to say "amen" to him. We should be ready to fulfill his plan, to do what he calls us to do each day. As we do we will discover him during the day.

The mystery of life grows richer and more beautiful the more we learn to allow God to be God and Jesus to be Lord. We are the creatures who have been called to play an intimate, personal role in his eternal plan. God has asked us to join him in making the world perfect. Our union with Jesus is completely dependent on our prayer with Jesus. It is in prayer that we discover his plans for us and his power in our lives. Listening in prayer is vital if that is to happen.

I have discovered that my life is so much fuller and richer now, not because I try harder but because I have learned how to stop trying and to allow God to take the lead in prayer. That's really all listening prayer is: allowing God to do the talking, which means I have to do the listening and the obeying. It seems that for me the most important thing I do each day is to be open to my Lord, to allow him to show me his plan and his ways, and to seek the courage to say "yes" to all that God wants.

The most solemn prayer that a Catholic offers when he attends the liturgy is the one which follows the priestly doxology. This prayer is called "the great amen." The amen signifies agreement with the priest's prayer of praise to the Lord. It signifies each person's yes to God. It is a statement of willingness to be one with Jesus in fulfilling the plan of the Father. Amen is our most important prayer in the liturgy and during our daily lives. But amen doesn't mean anything unless we have listened to God and are saying amen to something specific.

Television has a way of taking up a lot of our time. This is very important time and it is being used in a negative way. As we sit passively in front of the television, we allow ourselves to be subject to the anti-Christian values and the thinking of this world.

The kind of life presented by most television programs is far from the Father's plan for human life. And when we hear of disturbing events on the news, we get a negative outlook towards the world.

Several years ago, when I realized what television was doing to me, I decided not to give it up entirely but to give God equal time. I have found that giving God equal time means that I spin my wheels less, that I don't get caught up so much in activities that are frivolous and lead to nothing. My priorities change. God's values become more prominent in my life, and Jesus becomes more fully Lord of each day.

Now I consider it silly of me to make excuses for not praying. A daily prayer time which consists of a good deal of listening prayer enriches the whole day. It equips us with God's vision so that we can make good decisions and use our time well. The more I give time to reflecting and listening to God, the more I discover that God is like a winning coach—he is eager that his sons and daughters win at the game of life. God wants his sons and daughters to be winners in life. He wants us to prosper in every way so that we can be kingdom builders for him and with him. And it is only by listening to him that we can be effectively equipped for this.

Let us keep our eyes on Jesus. The image of Jesus at prayer before the Father should be before us each time we begin to pray. He listened to the Father and said amen to God's will even when it didn't agree with his own plans. Because of his listening and his amen, the entire world was set free. As we pray, listen, and say amen, a similar thing happens. We are set free. We are equipped to love and serve God.

It is absolutely vital for a Christian to spend time in listening prayer. For me it is each day, for others it may be less than that. God wants us to be eagles who ride the wind majestically rather than ducks who flap their wings incessantly. He wants us to listen and to soar.

FOUR

Keep Pentecost Alive!

THE PROCESS OF BUILDING THE CABIN that I share with several other priests put me in a position to meet a number of people who are truly living witnesses to the gospel of Christ. One was the owner of a sawmill. A friend and I had stopped in to find out if the man could furnish us with some rough cut cedar siding. I walked into the man's office and the first thing I noticed was a well-worn Bible on his desk.

"Do you read that book?" I asked him.

"Sure do," he replied. "Do you know what the two most important words in the Bible are?"

I wracked my brain. I could think of many important phrases in the Bible, but they all contained more than two words. My own candidate, "Jesus Christ is Lord," is four words. "Father, forgive them," is three. "This is my beloved son," is five.

"No," I replied at length. "What are the two most important words in the Bible?"

"Come and go," he said. "The secret is to come to Jesus to receive new life and then to go tell others about it."

I was very impressed by the wisdom of this simple man, the operator of a sawmill in an isolated, rural portion of northern Michigan. He kept his Christian faith alive by "coming" to Jesus and he was always willing to "go" tell anyone about the Lord. He was a living witness, a vessel from which the grace of Pentecost entered the lives of others.

Pentecost is kept alive by living witnesses, by people like you and me who are willing at any time to witness to anyone about the love of our Lord. Perhaps you have heard the expression, "You may be the only page of the New Testament that a particular person will ever read." That is so true. Many people won't even consider Christian faith an option for their lives unless they see Christians behaving in a truly Christian manner—as loving, serving, forgiving children of the Lord who are willing to talk about why they behave this way. Yet many good Christians are unwilling to open their mouths to communicate the invitation of the Good Shepherd to come and see the goodness of the Lord.

I recall one such incident many years ago. I had celebrated a liturgy welcoming the mother of a large farm family into the Catholic church. It was a wonderful celebration and the family asked me to come to their home after mass to celebrate further. After the supper dishes had been cleared, I sat for awhile at the kitchen table chatting with the woman and her husband.

While we were talking, Grace looked at me and said, "Father, you are the first person who invited me to become a Catholic."

I was stunned. This couple had raised a Catholic family. They had shared the ups and downs of life with many other Catholic families. They had entertained many active, committed Catholics in their home. The two priests who had preceded me as pastor had sat at that very table talking with this fine couple. Yet none of these people had ever invited this woman to enter into a full Christian life as a member of the church.

Why not? Because they had never learned the importance of being a witness to the Lord, a vessel of the grace of Pentecost. How tragic! Sharing our faith with others through evangelization is not an option. It is a command of the Lord given in Scripture and reiterated in our day by Pope Paul VI who said, "The church exists in order to evangelize." If you and I are not evangelizing, not inviting others to come and see, is the church alive in us?

I recalled my invitation to the woman. It really wasn't a big deal. I had scheduled a class for persons who wanted to know more about the church. I wanted to call her and extend a personal invitation, but I was involved with so many things that I really didn't have time. So I wrote Grace a note inviting her to join the class.

As I reflected about this I realized that Grace had been exposed over the years to the Lord. She had experienced the love of many Christians. She had brought her children up in the Christian faith. Many had been the moments when she had been touched with the grace of Pentecost—the grace of conversion. But here it was, a simple note written in haste, that became the vehicle God used to call her to the faith. That is a grace that comes from Pentecost.

Another person, a man named Dan, who is an expert in the computer field, had a similar moment. I knew Dan's wife. She was a fervent, active, Catholic lay woman. Most of Dan's friends were people who believed strongly in Christ and practiced their faith beautifully. One of these men was out one evening with Dan and put the question to him directly.

"Dan," he said, "I think you ought to join us. Your wife, your children, and all your friends are Catholics. I'm not going to bring it up again, but I want to challenge you. The faith makes so much sense and is such a big help in my life. You really ought to join us."

Five years later Dan got one of those notes from me and decided to take instructions. He believed what he heard and entered the church. Like Grace,

Dan was touched with the grace of Pentecost and became an active member of the Christian community.

During more than twenty years as a priest I have encountered many people like Grace and Dan. And I have concluded that effective evangelization is usually a community process. It is unusual for one person to bring another to faith in the Lord. It is rather the community of believers whose cumulative influence over a period of time touches the hearts of others. The Holy Spirit is the agent at work here. He alone can change hearts, and usually he does so as the individual sees the love of God being lived out in the lives of people he or she knows.

This is not to say that some people do not have a gift of evangelism. I do know people who are gifted in this way. They can evangelize with ease in public situations as well as private ones. But most people evangelize as they live the life of faith in community with others. However, even these people should always be open to the times when God wants us to evangelize another individual explicitly. Once in a while we do have the privilege to be his instrument to nudge someone on, to be used by God in his glorious work of attracting another to himself on an individual basis.

I know of nothing that gives greater pleasure than being in a situation where God is using me as a channel of his blessing of conversion. The more I hear the faith stories of others, the more I thank God for the blessing of a faith community like the Catholic church. In the church we have a diversity of talents and a wondrous organization which has proclaimed the gospel through the centuries, in spite of human weaknesses, to make us what we are today: a people of faith, a people with solid answers to offer a world in need. God works his purposes in us as a community.

Jesus is Lord of the church. We must never forget that. And as we realize more fully in our own lives that Jesus is Lord, his lordship over the entire community of the church grows stronger. As our awareness of his lordship grows, we find that we acquire new brothers and sisters, a whole communion of people, and in that communion we are bonded together in Christ by the Holy Spirit. This bonding—despite our diversity and the confusion we find in the church today—is the reason why the work of renewal in the Holy Spirit is so vital to the church in our day.

How does Jesus carry out his commitment to bring the whole world to the Father? The Scriptures make it clear that Jesus has a plan. When he was in the flesh he attracted men and women to himself and taught them the ways of his Father. And when they had come to understand, he told them to go forth and tell. The apostles were to live his word in community together and then pass this life on to others. This whole process is called tradition. It is the means by which the wondrous word of Jesus has been lived through the centuries. Living witnesses have gone forth to attract others to live for the same truths that Jesus lived for. That happens as individuals become one with the Lord Jesus and he becomes Lord of their lives. Then they become part of the community of believers which helps them remain faithful, bear fruit in his service, and spread the word of God to others.

Tradition is what produced the New Testament. It was not Jesus but the body of believers who wrote the New Testament. This is in keeping with his commission to go and make disciples. The church has done this in every century as it has responded to the Holy Spirit's activity. At some times the church has done this better than at other times, but the truth is that the Spirit has been and continues to be active in the church. How privileged we are to be part of this ongoing wave of human believers which passes on the gospel message and carries within it the saving message of Jesus.

What is the saving message? It is this: Jesus is Lord; Jesus is God's provision for salvation; by accepting him we become heirs to eternal life with God in heaven; and the day is coming when Jesus will come to earth again in all his glory and call all his followers to himself.

How do we live this message in our day? First of

all by following the precepts of the church: attend mass and confession and receive the Eucharist regularly; receive the other sacraments at appropriate times in your life; take advantage of the religious education programs for children and adults offered by your parish; obey the commandments of God—the ten commandments and the teachings of the church regarding morality.

Those basic things are the first level of living the kind of lives that faith in Jesus demands of us. But if we want Jesus to be truly Lord of our lives—Lord in deed as well as in word—we need to move to another level, a level that I call the grace of Pentecost.

When I think of Pentecost I think of Peter. He was a disciple of the Lord, an impetuous and sometimes cowardly man. When the grace of Pentecost entered his life, he was able to preach to large crowds and found that his words touched the hearts of many and led them to conversion. He prayed for people and they were instantly healed of their sickness; their sins were forgiven.

When I think of Pentecost I think of Mary. She said "amen" to God the Father's gift of the Holy Spirit and conceived Jesus, the word made flesh. Mary's whole life was a witness to her statement, "My soul proclaims the greatness of the Lord because God who is mighty has done great things for me." Little as she was, God could use her.

When I think of the grace of Pentecost I think of

Jesus coming forth from the Jordan anointed with the Holy Spirit. He proclaimed that the kingdom of God was at hand. On that day he began his long journey to Jerusalem where he died, rose from the dead, and assured the great victory of Christianity.

That wondrous grace of Pentecost that was so significant in the lives of Jesus, Peter, and Mary is passed on to us. It should be significant in our lives as well. The gift of the Holy Spirit is one of the wonders of God's grace, but it is a wonder that is a reality in every man and woman who proclaims with heart, word, and deed that Jesus Christ is Lord. Jesus anoints us with the Holy Spirit so that we might become holy; he also anoints us with the Spirit that we might become living witnesses. The power of the Spirit enables us to go forth and proclaim the gospel. As we do, we find that people are moved to follow the Lord, moved to turn away from the frivolous things of the world that lead to nothing, moved to follow the way of Jesus that leads to happiness and life everlasting.

The history of the Catholic church teaches us a great deal about how God works. Throughout our history the church has had bad leaders as well as good ones. Men who were weak and prone to greed have sometimes assumed and then abused positions of authority. Different members of the church have at times failed to respond fully to the call to love and service that God had given them. Yet, despite these problems, which at certain points in history were quite serious, God has been able to work his wonders through human vessels. There is no natural explanation for the presence of the church in our day. Every other human institution has gone by the wayside after only a few centuries. But the church carries on after two thousand years, in spite of human weakness.

This profound truth finds expression in a banner I once saw. "The church is not a museum for saints. It's a hospital for sinners." What this proves, I believe, is that God can work his wonders in our weakness. Paul said, "when I am weak, then I am strong" (2 Cor 12:10). What he meant was that at the times he recognized his weakness he was able to permit the Holy Spirit to work through him. Though he was incapable of doing a task that needed to be done, God was indeed capable. The same is true for individuals and for the church at large. When we recognize that we are weak, that we are sinful, that we are unable to fully be what God wants us to be and do what he wants us to do, we can be strong. If we have the humility to turn to God, to allow Jesus to be Lord of our lives, the power of Pentecost will come flooding into the church and she will be stronger than ever.

As I look at the difficulties in the church today, I see an opportunity to experience this. The church today is marked in many ways by confusion, by disagreement, by strife, or by apathy. Many of these instances are the result of human weakness and sin. The church is made up of very weak vessels. There is no question about that. But if in our weakness we turn to God, if we tell him that we are too weak to do it on our own, that we want Jesus to take his rightful place as Lord of the church, we can be strong again.

Remember that Jesus took on human nature and was born, lived, and died as a man. We call this the incarnation. The incarnational principle shows us that God did not desire to bypass human weakness as he came to bring salvation to the earth. Rather, he worked in human weakness. I am not saying that Jesus was weak spiritually. But he inhabited a human body and was subject to the bodily weaknesses, to the temptations that we are all subject to. The men and women he called to spread his message and build his church were weak. And this continues today. Jesus is willing to work through me and through you. We are all weak human beings, but the Lord is very willing to work through us to build his kingdom.

How can this be? I discovered that it is the gift of the Holy Spirit—the gift of Pentecost—that brings this about. It is divine power, the power of the Spirit, that God uses to dwell in human nature and to make human beings useful for his kingdom. The gift of the Holy Spirit has been given to me so that I can carry on the work of Jesus in my day. The call on my life is to be a sacrament, a channel of his grace, and he can use my human weakness in order to carry on his work.

I continue to stumble, to fall short of God's perfect plan for me; I continue to be weak and to sin. But I have learned to be humble enough to come back to the Lord, to ask Jesus once again to become Lord of my life. When I do, God renews his grace within me and enables me to carry on. He is never stopped by our weakness. The will of God will be done in spite of our weakness. And if we recognize this and are humble about it, God's work will progress smoothly in our lives.

As I mentioned before, I learned another way of expressing this truth: I love the church, wrinkles and all. I have always loved the ideal church, the church of my dreams, the church that is everything that God wants it to be. Unfortunately, because of human weakness, the church isn't even close to that point. So the Lord told me to love the real church, wrinkles, warts, pimples, and all. As I have grown in my love for Jesus, I have learned to love the church because Jesus identified himself with the church. It isn't enough for me to love the ideal Lord; he wants me to love his bride, the church. He wants me to see in the church a place where I can live and dwell in his word, where I can be part of his mission being carried on in the world today. It is in the church that

I have the great opportunity to live the grace of Pentecost.

I have been a channel to bring salvation to others. It is clear that I am weak and that my plans usually accomplish very little. It is clear that it was a mistake for me to look upon the Holy Spirit as the one who would be *my* helper as I took on the tasks of priest and bishop. The Pope said it clearly: the Holy Spirit is the one who carries on the saving work of Jesus. Human beings are to assist him and to submit to his plans and his working. The Spirit of God works through human beings who are willing to say "amen" as Mary did to his plan and his way. When we do, the Spirit moves out in wondrous power and God's kingdom is built. As men and women say "amen" to the Spirit, the grace of Pentecost continues to glow and inflame the lives of others.

The gift of the Holy Spirit, the gift of Pentecost, is the power that builds God's kingdom and sustains it throughout the ages. It is clear then that if we are to be sensitive to the Holy Spirit, we must be attentive to the Lord in prayer. His movements are often subtle. But it is important that we recognize the moments when he prompts us to share the gospel of salvation with another. It is so important that we have lives steeped in prayer so that we can recognize those moments.

I've been talking about some of the implications

of the gift of Pentecost; now I'd like to tell you about some of my own experiences of Pentecost, what God did for me as I have said "amen" to the Holy Spirit's manifestations of power in the charismatic renewal.

FIVE

The Paraclete of Jesus

MY FIRST MEETING WITH POPE PAUL VI was a key moment for the charismatic renewal and a key moment in my life. I have a photograph that recalls the time when he met with eleven leaders of the Catholic renewal. Archbishop James Hayes of Halifax, Nova Scotia, Canada, and I had been asked to lead a group of lay charismatic leaders to meet with the Holy Father. We didn't realize until later that Cardinal Suenens had worked very hard behind the scenes to make that meeting possible.

It was a distinct honor for representatives of a new and somewhat controversial movement to meet with the Holy Father. What I remember most about that meeting was not the trappings of papal authority but rather the special light in his eyes and the look of grace on his face as he read a statement to us. The statement expressed the hope that he saw in the new "spiritual movement" that we were part of.

It is interesting to note that Paul VI did not refer to our movement as charismatic renewal because he believed that charisms were applicable to the entire church and he did not want to see the term applied only to one segment of the church. At one time this caused some concern among participants in the charismatic renewal who felt that because he didn't refer to us by name he wasn't really understanding or endorsing what God was doing among us. However, whenever he addressed groups of charismatics—which he did several times—it was very clear that he understood full well what God was doing among us and that he approved of it wholeheartedly.

Paul VI's statement to us that day was very encouraging. When he finished reading it, he looked at Archbishop Hayes and me and said, "Discernment is above all the role of bishops." At that moment I rejoiced because I had discerned that God was indeed working in power among Catholic charismatics, drawing them closer to his heart and closer to the church. I concluded from his statement that the Holy Father saw in the movement the same things I saw. I also saw in his statement a great challenge for me to continue that role of discernment, of striving to understand what the Holy Spirit is doing in the world today.

The call for me to relate more to the Holy Spirit was upon me. I was called to be one of those charged with the responsibility for providing discernment about whether the work that God was doing among his people through the charismatic renewal was truly for the church and in keeping with God's plans for renewal in our day. The Holy Father was reminding me that bishops have a responsibility to provide spiritual discernment to the laity; but I knew that I was incapable of doing that effectively without receiving the wisdom of the Holy Spirit. That was one of the many moments of my life when I was challenged to learn how to relate to the Holy Spirit in a fuller way.

It was almost as profound a realization of God's call on my life as when I had received another call from Pope Paul VI. In 1968 he wrote me a letter asking me to serve the church as an auxiliary bishop to Bishop Allen J. Babcock, ordinary of the Diocese of Grand Rapids. I remember being frozen for a moment after reading those words. I was overwhelmed by the prospect of being a bishop: I saw it as an honor far greater than I deserved and as a responsibility that exceeded my natural abilities. Yet, it was clear that in God's providence I was called to take on those responsibilities. I had to take some time to discern whether to say yes or no to that challenge. Although it is unusual for a priest to decline to serve as a bishop, it is permissible. In a moment of prayer I was led to go before my own bishop and to explain to him the many reasons I had for saying no.

Bishop Babcock sat and listened very kindly to my recitation of my weaknesses and shortcomings. When I finished he said, "There's only one thing you forgot—the Holy Spirit. Bishops need the Holy Spirit, and they have a unique claim on the Spirit's grace."

That simple wisdom sustained me often in the ensuing years, and through it I was able to give a heartfelt yes to the church's invitation to serve as a bishop. Bishop Babcock planted a seed in my heart that day and that seed has produced much fruit, not only in my own life but in the lives of many people. I have come to appreciate that the Holy Spirit is the source of power that each Christian needs to live the vocation that Christ has called us to. I discovered this in a unique way when I was asked to serve as a bishop in the church.

Along the way I have learned a number of lessons about relating to the Holy Spirit. A key discovery was when I realized that the Holy Spirit is a real person of the Blessed Trinity. It is difficult for some people to realize this. We can relate to God the Father because we know what a human father is. And we can picture a divine Father because we see Jesus relating to the Father in the Gospels. He called the Father *abba*, an Aramaic word that is best translated into English as "daddy." Jesus related to God as "daddy," and he tells us to do the same.

Similarly, we can relate to Jesus, the Son, because

he was a human being as well as God. We can picture him as a baby in Bethlehem, a boy in Nazareth, a young man preaching in the synagogues and city squares. I once saw a scene in a television movie that showed Jesus and the apostles playing a game together. As I watched that I was even more able to get in touch with the human being who is also my Lord and my God. I am certain that Jesus did play the popular games of the day with his disciples once in a while. How human! How easy to identify with!

But the Holy Spirit is a different story. The word of God presents the third person of the Trinity as wind, tongues of fire, and other elements that are hard to identify with. The only time the Holy Spirit takes on a form recognizable to us is as a bird. It's hard for humans to have a relationship with a bird. So we are handicapped in our relationship with the Spirit of God. But this doesn't need to be. The Holy Spirit is someone we can call upon as a person and respond to as a person.

Since the day that Bishop Babcock planted the seed of recognizing the Spirit in my life, I have learned a number of lessons about relating to him. The first is what I call the "epiclesis" principle. Epiclesis means that we should be invoking the Holy Spirit often. And in fact we do in the prayers of the church. This practice finds its roots in the creation story in the Scriptures. There we find that in the midst of chaos the Spirit of God hovered over the water, and the word of God was issued into the chaos and it became a created world. This pattern has been repeated through the centuries: times of chaos serve as creative moments for God. The lesson for us is clear: when there is chaos in our lives or in our world, we should turn to the Holy Spirit to discern the word of God and when the word is issued and followed, God moves in power to create something new, profound, and lasting.

We find this is true of the annunciation. Mary is told that she will conceive God's own Son. This news troubles her and produces a certain amount of chaos in her life. She is young, engaged but not yet living with her husband; an apparent illegitimate pregnancy could cause untold trouble for Mary and her husband. Yet this young woman hears the word of God and is faithful to it. As a result, God sends the Spirit upon her and she conceives a child who becomes the Savior of all humanity.

We find another such creative moment on the day of Pentecost. The disciples were huddled together in the upper room with Mary and several of their friends—men and women. They were a weak, fearful bunch. It was a chaotic situation. But they remained faithful to the word they had received and the Holy Spirit came upon them, empowering them to proclaim the good news of the lordship of Jesus. The church was born that day and has gone on to change the course of human history as God's kingdom has spread throughout the world.

The church preserves the epiclesis principle every time the liturgy is celebrated. We still bring to the altar the bread and wine which represent the elements of daily human life with all its chaos. In obedience to the word of God, we ask the Holy Spirit to come upon that bread and wine and thus it becomes the body and blood of Jesus. Each time this creative moment occurs, Jesus comes anew to his people, to feed us and strengthen us to do the work of the kingdom of God.

In each of these instances we call upon the Holy Spirit because that is the way God continues to work his wonders on the earth. It is clear, therefore, that Christians should invoke the Holy Spirit at times of chaos—times of illness, danger, confusion, helplessness. We invoke the Holy Spirit, seek God's word for that moment, and almost inevitably we will see that God will use us as he used Mary to make moments of chaos into creative moments, moments when Jesus will establish God's kingdom more fully among us.

My introduction to this was the realization that problems are usually opportunities; that today's seeds are tomorrow's flowers. If we call upon the Holy Spirit, if we seek God's light in the situation, we will very often find a word from God that brings some kind of order to the situation and we find that God indeed works through it in power. I have applied this often in my life and I have found that I don't need to fear problems. I have the Holy Spirit and God's word to help me get through them and discover the creative moment that God has in mind.

A deeper discernment of this role of the Holy Spirit in our lives comes from a study of Jesus' teaching about the Holy Spirit as Paraclete. This is the one situation in the Scriptures where the Holy Spirit is discussed in human terms. In John's Gospel Jesus gives the Holy Spirit the title of Paraclete. This is a very interesting title because we still today use the Greek word that Jesus used: *paracletos* means the one who has been called upon. We do not have an adequate word in English to describe this function, but it does imply a person, a person we can call upon to come and help us. A paraclete is a helper.

To this day in the sacrament of confirmation the church calls upon the Holy Spirit to be a helper and guide to those who are confirmed. It is my belief that we should constantly be calling upon the Holy Spirit to be our helper and guide. Call upon him in times of temptation, times of trouble, times of fear or confusion or doubt. God has given him to us as our helper; let's not be afraid to ask him for his help! When we do we can experience the victory of the resurrection in our lives.

The constant quest of the Christian is to be able to determine when it is right to call upon the Holy Spirit and when it is right for us to use our own efforts. Learning when to call upon the Holy Spirit is a central factor in learning how to live a more God-like life. I like the expression used by a brother priest who said that discerning how to live with the Holy Spirit is like riding the wind. The test of a mature Christian is learning when to flap our wings and when to ride the wind of the Holy Spirit. This is not an easy question to answer; it is something that we learn how to do better as we grow older in our walk with the Lord. But it is important to keep it in mind, to constantly ask ourselves whether to flap our wings in this situation or to ride the wind by relaxing and letting the Lord work.

I have discovered five functions of a paraclete that help us know when to call upon the Holy Spirit:

1. Invoke the Holy Spirit when we need assistance. This implies our recognition of our weaknesses: we know we need help.

I find that it takes us a long time to overcome the old habit of turning to the Holy Spirit last instead of first. But when we learn to invoke the Holy Spirit as soon as we recognize a moment of weakness or chaos, they become moments of opportunity, moments when God can create.

For example, I recall a time not so long ago when I responded to a situation with anger. I thought it was righteous anger, the kind of anger that moves toward a positive solution of a problem rather than being a destructive, consuming anger. In a moment of examination of conscience in the evening, I faced the fact that my anger was not righteous at all. I had given in to weakness and I had responded in a selfish way toward the other person involved. In my consternation I turned to the Lord. I invoked the Holy Spirit, begging God for the gift of meekness, the gift Jesus exemplified on the cross: responding to anger and violence with love and forgiveness. I learned that night and in the following days how much I needed this gift, and God turned my consternation into joy as I began to realize that God was giving me this gift of meekness because I had invoked the Holy Spirit.

2. We invoke the Holy Spirit to enable us. Many times in the course of daily life we find ourselves challenged beyond our abilities. This can happen at work, at school, in our relationships with others, or even during prayer. The Holy Spirit is the one sent by God to enable us to stand strong during such times. He is always depicted as the courage of God. We can face the storms of life not only with our own strength but also with God's strength.

Christians are constantly confronted with situations that would seem to overwhelm us. God often stretches us beyond our breaking point, but with the help of the Holy Spirit we find that we don't break. Such stress moments, when we invoke the Holy Spirit, are the growth moments in our lives.

I find that I often call upon the Holy Spirit when anxiety is beginning to overwhelm me. That can happen often, and in my life it has. But when I call upon the Holy Spirit to help me, he reminds me of the words of Jesus: "I am the vine, you are the branches; without me you can do nothing." We must stay attached to him. As we do, we share in his resurrection victory in the situations that would otherwise overwhelm us.

3. Invoke the Holy Spirit in times of confusion. Jesus called the Holy Spirit the advocate and the Spirit of truth. The Holy Spirit is our advocate, the one who leads us into truth. It makes sense, therefore, to turn to him for a dose of divine truth during times when we are confused or beginning to doubt. The church teaches us about seven gifts of the Holy Spirit. Four of these are the Spirit's helps in times of confusion: he gives us wisdom, understanding, knowledge, and right judgment.

One instance of this kind of help happened when the diocese determined that it was time to find someone else to manage a nursing home for the elderly that we had operated for a number of years. This was a very difficult problem and although I was charged with the responsibility of solving it, I had no idea how to do it. I kept putting it off. One morning as I was praying the Lord impressed upon me the thought that I should call upon the advocate, that this was the day that my confusion would be dispelled in this area.

I obeyed that prompting and invoked the Spirit.

Then I got on the telephone and called a sister who lived in a city a long distance away. She had already told us that she was not interested in the position because of other opportunities in her life. But I called her anyway and as we talked she told me that that very day she had determined to make a decision about which way the Lord was calling her to turn in her life. The Holy Spirit had operated to dispose her to consider our offer at the same time that he had stirred me up to talk with her. During the conversation the sister agreed to come and be interviewed, and she did indeed serve as administrator of the home. During her time of service, she brought a number of God's blessings to many people and solved many of our problems.

I will never forget that day. I had begged the Holy Spirit, the advocate, to plead God's cause in my heart and in the sister's heart. And it worked.

4. We invoke the Holy Spirit when we struggle with evil. It is proper during times of temptation, and most especially in times of struggle with evil power, that we invoke the Holy Spirit. In those times the Spirit's work is to make Jesus present to us. This makes sense because Jesus came to overcome evil and establish the kingdom of God.

I remember one time when I was walking down a street, I encountered a man who had the following slogan emblazoned on his t-shirt: "Booze is the answer; I don't remember the question." It was so clear to me that evil was being projected. There was no good news in that slogan, nor in the appearance of the shirt. It was a black t-shirt with white letters. It looked as evil as the sentiments it projected.

Is life worth living? The answer is Jesus. He is the one who makes life worth living. And he sends us his Holy Spirit in order that he might be present in our lives. As we experience more of him in our lives, we are filled with his victory over evil, we are strengthened in our relationship with God, and we receive the power to live fruitfully in God's kingdom. The Holy Spirit gives us what we need to oppose evil with courage and strength. He enables us to look into the face of sin and not be subject to it.

The beautiful prayer of St. Francis reminds us of the power the Spirit brings to help us respond to this part of life:

Where there is injury, let me bring pardon.
Where there is despair, let me bring hope.
Where there is hatred, let me bring love.

The peace of God, the hope of God, the love of God are the answers to so many of the moments of evil that confront us during our lives. And the Holy Spirit is sent by Jesus to activate us so that we can live in his peace, his love, and overcome the strife and the hatred that the devil would try to sow in our lives.

5. We invoke the Holy Spirit in times of fear. The Greeks used to call upon a paraclete to stir up the troops before a battle. His job was to help them overcome their fear of the enemy and to call upon their own great inner strength so that they could march into battle full of vigor.

Fear can have a paralyzing effect on human beings. Even very good people are afraid of what others might think if they make a mistake. When we learn to invoke the Holy Spirit in moments of fear, we can step out in boldness and receive the power of the Lord to proclaim his kingdom and extend his reign.

This picture of the Holy Spirit is so clear in the battle between David and Goliath. I once heard a preacher say that Saul looked upon Goliath and reacted in fear, saying, "He is too big to kill." But David, full of the Spirit of God, looked at Goliath and said, "He is too big to miss." That is the way that we can look at any fear-causing situation. We can confront any situation with God's power operating in our lives, knowing that we have the victory because the Holy Spirit is with us.

The Holy Spirit comes into our lives in a profound way in the sacraments of baptism and confirmation. Each individual Christian has a choice to make. We can allow the Spirit to lie dormant in our lives or to come alive in us. If we learn to invoke the Holy Spirit regularly, we will find that we can relate to him as a person. Thus we experience the grace of Pentecost in our own lives. The Holy Spirit has a place in our lives each day. He is our paraclete, someone we can relate to, someone we can call upon to help us, someone who helps us say with our lips and our lives that Jesus Christ is Lord!

SIX

The Face of the Holy Spirit

WHEN YOU HAVE THE PRIVILEGE of visiting the Holy Land, you discover that Jesus becomes so much more real for you. When you see the land where he lived, you see *how* he lived, and this tells you something about him that you might not otherwise have learned. Once when I was visiting the Holy Land I had the privilege of staying in the Monastery of the Annunciation in Nazareth. The priest who lives there, Father John Leonard, was raised in my hometown. Later he had been welcomed into the Maronite church and was educated and ordained in the Holy Land. He was serving as the priest-chaplain of this monastery of sisters and as such had invited me to spend some time there.

During one of our conversations he told me about some of the aspects of our faith that are brought out more fully in the life of the many Orthodox churches and what are called the Oriental Rites of the Catholic church—the Melchites, the Armenian, the Maronite, and several others.

Father Leonard told me about the tradition of icon theology in the Eastern Rites. Icons are art objects—usually paintings. They are created by artists who pray as they work. The intention of icons is to depict God living and working through the life of the saint being depicted—to show divinity working in humanity.

One aspect of icon theology that Father Leonard told me about is a very rich understanding of God the Father. Eastern Christians see God as a Father who extends himself to the human race in order to bring us to himself. Imagine a painting of God reaching out to you. One of his arms is Jesus, the word made flesh, the Savior who draws us to the Father. The other arm is the Holy Spirit, the One who dwells within us in order to sanctify us, to bring us to new life, and to draw us to the Father.

"God wants to embrace us with both arms," Father Leonard said. "But many Christians in the Western church act like God has a withered arm." Now, my friend had grown up in the church before Vatican II and did not fully realize the many stirrings of the Holy Spirit among Western Catholics in the years since he had left his native land. But his point did remind me that members of the church are becoming more fully aware of the key role that the Holy Spirit plays in the world. As Catholics become more aware of the fact that God does not have a withered arm, we grow more quickly in God's kingdom ways.

In the Acts of the Apostles, the accounts of what happened immediately after Pentecost are recorded, and we see the power of the Holy Spirit at work in the lives of these early Christians. The word which the Greek writers of Acts used for the Spirit's power was *dynamis,* a word that is the root of our words dynamite, dynamo, and dynamic. This word speaks of explosive power—not destructive power but creative power. It is like what happens to a flower in the springtime. It seems to take so long for the stem of a flower to grow; then the bud appears and seems to grow slowly. Suddenly, in less than a day, the bud opens and the flower is apparent in all its beauty.

The power of the Holy Spirit is like that. It can erupt very suddenly and create works of beauty among the sons and daughters of God. As I reflected on how often Luke uses this word in the book of Acts, I found myself searching for some kind of word that we use today that speaks of the impact of the Holy Spirit in our lives. The best word I've been able to find is gusto. Gusto describes that blooming, vital kind of exuberance that we experience from time to time. Gusto gives us newness of life. God sends us his Holy Spirit so that we might live our

Christian lives with gusto: so that we might know new life, share in new life, grow in new life, and spread new life to others around us.

The new life is the life of God's kingdom. The Gospels remind us of this by offering us reflections on the nature of the kingdom of God, the reign of God. When we learn how to allow the Holy Spirit to touch our lives and to bring newness, the kingdom of God reigns with us.

I was very gratified to learn that shortly after I had my discussion with my priest friend in Nazareth, the church renewed the way that priests give absolution during the sacrament of reconciliation. The new rite uses the following prayer: "God the Father of mercy, through the death and resurrection of Jesus, reconciled the world to himself, and he sends the Holy Spirit for the forgiveness of sins. May God grant you pardon and peace. Through the ministry of the church I absolve you from your sins in the name of the Father, and of the Son, and of the Holy Spirit."

That prayer is one very profound way that God reaches out his arms to embrace the sinner and to give peace and newness of life. It is a good example of how the Holy Spirit comes and the kingdom of God grows within us.

I believe that the most significant statement about the Holy Spirit in recent years was the statement of Pope Paul VI in his exhortation *Evangelii Nuntiandi* (Evangelization in the Modern World). This great document discusses how Catholics are to spread the gospel of Jesus in the world today. One of his points is this: the Holy Spirit is the principle agent of evangelization. This means that God is the one who does the work and that we are his helpers. When I let the concept sink in, my outlook on the work of the Holy Spirit changed completely. I began to see that God's plan is not that I make my plans and call upon the Holy Spirit to help me achieve them, but rather that I strive to be in contact with the Holy Spirit in such a way that his objectives for me will become my own objectives. The idea is that I follow his promptings and then ask him for his help so that I can carry them out.

When I am sensitive to the Holy Spirit in my own life, I recognize his action in the hearts of others. Pope Paul's letter teaches that while the Holy Spirit is active by prompting the heart of the evangelizer, he is also active by preparing the heart of the one to be evangelized. I recall so many moments in my life when I followed a prompting of the Holy Spirit to step out in a particular way, and I found that God had already prepared the heart of the other person. That is kingdom power: the Holy Spirit brings newness to my life and he brings newness to your life and when we come in contact with each other, we sense something of the dynamism of God's love and power.

If we are going to relate properly to the Holy

Spirit we have to be sensitive to his promptings; we have to be aware also that he is preparing the hearts of others to be receptive. The most significant single word that can be said about the Holy Spirit is surprise. There is no way that we can predict how, where, when, and why the Holy Spirit will move. But when we have the sensitivity to the role of the Holy Spirit, we often experience the wonderful surprises that bring newness of life.

How do we grow in this kind of openness? One way is to ask the Holy Spirit the following questions very explicitly every day: "Are you trying to say anything to me today? Is there something you want me to know or something you want me to do?" I ask this question during my prayer time each day, and I find that very often the Spirit will give me insights that will be useful to people I am in contact with. This has happened so often to me that I now consider it to be an ordinary way that the Holy Spirit works.

One example of this is an insight I once had about the problem of anxiety. I was struck with the realization that anxiety usually results from fear about tomorrow. I had heard so often that the doctrine of grace is such that God gives us the grace to follow him one day at a time. He is the "I am," not the "I will be." So we need to have confidence that his power and love are with us today and that they will be with us when tomorrow comes. We need not be afraid about tomorrow.

That insight became a special consolation for me. I shared it a number of times during homilies and personal conversations, and I have heard that it helped many people overcome fear about the future. They were able to surrender their anxiety to the Holy Spirit who conquered it for them.

Another way that we can be more open to the working of the Holy Spirit is when we open our lives to Jesus in the Eucharist. When we receive the Eucharist, it is important that we keep in mind that we are coming to Jesus who, with the Father, sends us the Holy Spirit. When we approach Jesus we should feel welcome to ask God for the gift that we feel we most need to become kingdom builders. When we do this, we have a sense that we are moving in God's will and that the Holy Spirit will make better use of us as kingdom builders. This is an exciting way to live!

When the church renewed the prayers of the mass, she prescribed an epiclesis—an invocation of the Holy Spirit—to be made during the prayers of consecration. She also prescribed an amnesis. This is a specific invocation of the Holy Spirit to bring us unity, to bring us together and help us be one people. The Spirit's role to unify is one that we need to reflect on, particularly as we see the variety of gifts that God gives to his people, the church.

When I was studying for the priesthood, I had the

privilege of studying for four years at the college of the Propagation of the Faith in Rome. The seminary was attended by men from forty-five nations. Caucasian men like me were a minority, and we grew to appreciate the variety within the human race and to see the variety within the kingdom of Jesus Christ. It was such a rich experience, but what impressed me the most was that despite our differences, we were one in Jesus Christ, especially when we stood together around the table of the Lord. When I left I had a profound sense of loss because my experience back in the United States would not be as rich.

Fortunately, God has given me the privilege of traveling to places like Trinidad, where people from many different races have come together through immigration and intermarriage. When these people are fired with the unity of the Holy Spirit, as are members of the charismatic renewal in Trinidad, the unity in the midst of racial and cultural diversity is truly phenomenal.

Christians in the affluent Western nations need to realize how rich and diverse is the body of Christ. When we realize that we are such a small part of the entirety of God's plan, we understand how the Holy Spirit is active worldwide. As the Holy Spirit is received, he makes a unified family out of us. It is very important for us to realize that the Holy Spirit loves variety and works within it to build the kingdom of Jesus. This is the basis for the pluralism that we see in God's kingdom. I like to compare this with a flower garden: God is a master gardener and his garden contains flowers of every shape, color, and size imaginable. We are his flowers and as we recognize the variety of flowers in the garden in which he has planted us, our unity grows. God doesn't want just roses or tulips. He loves variety, yet our unity runs much deeper than does color, or race, or creed.

After some seventeen years of reflecting on the role of the Holy Spirit, I thought I knew just about everything there was to know about the third person of the Trinity. Then one day while I was praying I was prompted to ask God this question: "Why didn't you give the Holy Spirit a face?" I was recalling how Scripture depicts the Spirit as breath, wind, fire, water, and a dove. And these are the symbols that Christians use to call to mind the Spirit's action in our lives. But if the Holy Spirit is a person, it seemed so much more appropriate that he have a human face as do the Son and the Father.

"Why doesn't the Holy Spirit have a face?" The question remained with me for some time. The first inspiration that came to me was that sometimes a face gets in the way. It was as if God was saying to me, "If you're looking for a face, you'll never find the Spirit, for I've sent the Spirit to dwell in your heart. Don't look outwardly for the Spirit; look within your own heart."

This answer satisfied me for some time. Later I was visiting a retirement home where elderly sisters who had served the church well were living out their last days on earth. I told one of the sisters about the answer that God gave me about why the Holy Spirit doesn't have a face.

"Do you want to know how I pray to the Holy Spirit?" she asked me. "I pray like this: 'You haven't got a body, so use mine.'"

As I looked at that sister I was overwhelmed with understanding and with joy. I realized how much the Holy Spirit wants to use my body and my face. As I looked at her, I realized that the Holy Spirit was really there. Her face and her entire demeanor exhibited those qualities that Paul calls the fruit of the Spirit: peace, joy, patience, kindness, goodness, gentleness, and self-control.

The Lord had taught me two very profound things about his Holy Spirit: the Spirit dwells within me in order to build me up spiritually; and he uses me in order to build his kingdom in others. If I am alert about the working of the Holy Spirit in my life, he can use my body and my face as his own. If I can allow him to take over within me, then I can project the love, the peace, and the joy that only the Holy Spirit can give to this world that cries out in anguish.

I acted upon this insight by observing the faces of God's people as they came to Sunday liturgy to hear the word of God and to receive the Eucharist. I realized how the face of the Holy Spirit is with the church. As I looked at so many different faces of so many different believers, I saw his face and I rejoiced. This is what Paul meant when he said that Jesus is the head and we are the body. It is the Spirit who makes us one body under one Lord.

There are many ways that we minister to one another in the power of the Holy Spirit. One that is especially apparent in the church today is healing. I'd like to discuss that a bit in the next chapter.

SEVEN

Healed to Heal

"DON'T YOU BELIEVE in the power of your ordination?"

The woman's eyes communicated the question even more strongly than her voice. She was perplexed by my hesitation about praying with her for God to heal another person's physical problem. I found myself immediately confronted with a question about my own faith. Did I really believe that God could heal?

Of course I did. The Catholic tradition is full of healing—not only the spectacular healing episodes like those at Lourdes, France, or those surrounding the lives of great saints. But Catholics believe in healing because we have seen it throughout the ages. Our healing tradition began when Peter prayed for the blind man at the Beautiful Gate of Jerusalem as recorded early in the Acts of the Apostles. And this tradition has been passed down from generation to generation ever since. But could I, a simple bishop, ask God to suspend the natural order and deliver someone from a medical condition that the doctors couldn't treat?

The woman had a good point: the charism of healing is often associated with the grace that God confers on a priest with the sacrament of Holy Orders. I decided to step out in faith, pray for the person, and see what would happen. To my amazement, the person got much better. I was even more amazed sometime later when I decided to join a group of lay people who were praying for a lady who was afflicted with multiple sclerosis. She was at a point in her life when she could no longer deal with the disease. She was suffering from severe depression and she asked members of a parish prayer group to pray with her for strength. As the mother of six children and an active member of the parish, she knew that she could not continue without God's help.

We prayed for her and we were surprised to find that she no longer had to deal with the weakness. Shortly after the prayer session the disease went into remission and has stayed in remission for ten years. The woman claims that God has healed her and she now spends most of her free time praying for and serving the needs of others. She knows what God has done for her and she knows that he will heal the afflictions of anyone who comes to him in faith.

That healing is one of the most dramatic ones that I have ever personally witnessed. Seeing God work in such power helped me to believe fully in the power of my ordination. Since then I've learned to also believe in the power of Baptism, Confirmation, and Matrimony. Like Holy Orders, these sacraments fill the faithful Christian with God's grace which then opens their lives to many kinds of divine power. These graces are then nourished by the Holy Eucharist and Reconciliation which make God's grace grow in our lives on an ongoing basis.

Each of the sacraments is an encounter with the living God for those who receive it. And those of us who receive the sacraments in faith can then go forth to mediate the grace we have received in the lives of others.

I have seen God answer prayers for healing quickly and dramatically many times during the past ten years. But there have been other times when God has chosen not to answer the prayers with a healing. Two episodes stand out very clearly in my mind. The first was when the wife of a very fine man who is now a close friend was diagnosed as having terminal cancer. The whole family was upset, but they weren't so sure that they wanted me to pray over the woman. Finally I prevailed upon them to allow me to minister the sacraments of Reconciliation and Anointing of the Sick. The latter sacrament was conferred during a home mass and the family and friends of the woman joined together to pray for her.

We followed this by having two people from the prayer group go to the woman's house every week to pray with her and ask the Lord to heal her. I joined them as often as possible. The Lord did not heal her body. She died the very week that the doctor had predicted. But although healing did not occur as we had asked, we found that God's power was manifest in a number of ways. The woman was filled with hope because she knew that her husband, her children, and her friends were praying with her and that God was strengthening them.

The funeral was one of the most beautiful liturgical services I have ever had the joy of presiding at. Many people were touched at that ceremony. Subsequently many people have been led to conversion and newness of life because of the witness of this holy woman's life and death. God answered our prayers for healing, not in the way we expected but in powerful, dramatic ways nonetheless.

A similar thing happened with a little boy who was afflicted with a brain tumor. We prayed often with him and for him. Our faith was strong because we were so sure that God would heal this innocent little boy. God chose instead to prepare him for a holy and beautiful death, one which was an inspiration to many people. Many people grew in faith as we prayed for that boy and saw him pass on to the Lord in a most holy, dignified way. God had answered our prayers!

I have prayed with others for healing and I have experienced God's healing touch in my own life. One day God dealt with a back problem that I suffered from as I prayed following the celebration of the Holy Eucharist. That prayer was offered at a mass during which many people were having an extended period of praise, thanksgiving, and jubilant rejoicing. As I joined them I asked the Lord to extend his healing touch to my pain-ridden back.

"Jesus," I prayed, "your body and blood are now in my bloodstream, your divine power is present physically as well as spiritually. I ask you to heal my back. If you choose not to heal it, then please give me the grace to endure the pain. Please help me to understand how the pain can serve the ministry you have called me to. I leave it in your hands."

As we left the church that day I noticed that my back was free of pain for the first time in weeks. The pain has never returned. So I learned that prayer for healing in the context of the sacramental life of the church is very powerful prayer. The Holy Eucharist is a sacrament of spiritual healing, and I have seen it affect spiritual healing as well.

Each of these experiences has taught me a lesson about healing. But the most dramatic lesson I have learned occurred at one of the national charismatic renewal conferences at the University of Notre Dame. The conference organizers decided to feature a healing service. I went to that healing service with many questions. At that time I did not know how to respond to these claims of healing in the charismatic renewal. I wanted to be open, but I was very suspicious.

One of the things I noticed was that exuberant praise of God always accompanies prayer for healing. The leaders exhorted the people to increasingly fervent prayers. They reminded me of cheerleaders, and at first I thought that they were trying to force testimonies of healing by producing mass hysteria.

Things improved as people came forward to pray at the microphone. The prayers for healing were simple and sincere, the kind of humble prayer that had attracted me to charismatics in the first place. But suddenly someone came to the microphone and began announcing healings that he claimed were occurring in the assembly. He described the persons and where they were sitting.

I was upset by this. "How," I asked myself, "can people know what God is doing? This is manipulation." I grew more and more uneasy as the service continued. Later, however, God began dealing with me. I woke up in the middle of the night, still troubled by what had happened earlier. Suddenly this thought occurred to me: "You do not object to cheerleading during a football game. In fact, you enjoy it. Why do you object to people being exuberant about praising God? What's wrong with leaders encouraging people to praise God?"

That was, I decided, a very good question. God certainly was more worthy of praise than football or basketball players. The things God did had lasting consequences. They concerned matters of life and death. And when God worked in power to restore life and health, I should not object if people are happy about it. If they want to jump and shout when God heals someone, that should be fine with me, even if I choose not to do that.

The next day I met a woman who asked if I remembered her. She was the next-door neighbor of some relatives whom I had visited on several occasions. She told me that one of the words of revelation about God healing someone—one of the messages that had so disturbed me the night before—had concerned her. "I am the lady who had trouble seeing," she said. "But God healed me last night, just like the speaker said."

I was stunned. It was as if God had grabbed me by the lapels and said, "Look, maybe you should believe your people instead of suspecting them."

A few months later I was giving a talk at a city some three hundred miles from Notre Dame. A lady met me at the door and said, "Bishop, I am one of those who was healed at the meeting at Notre Dame. I am the one who was wearing a red skirt and suffered from a kidney ailment."

"How do you know you were healed?" I asked.

She told me that the pain left the night of the healing service, but she didn't tell anyone that she had been healed until after being examined by her doctor. "My doctor cannot explain it," she said. "But my incurable kidney ailment has been healed."

God had shattered my doubts one after another. I then began to reflect on healing and I realized that physical and spiritual healing is an important part of the ministry of Jesus and therefore is part of the mission of the church. I recalled how during my youth people asked God to heal them as they prayed novenas. I had also visited the famous shrine at Lourdes and I had seen the healing services conducted there. As I reflected on this solid grounding in Catholic tradition, I realized that healing is not a result of where one is prayed for or who does the praying. Rather, it is a result of the disposition of the human heart. When God's people look upon him as a loving father who has their best interests in mind, when they approach him in prayer with love and faith filling their hearts and lives, God can and will heal.

I suspect that there is something very natural about the healing ministry. A number of doctors have told me that a majority of their patients suffer from illnesses that have psychological origins rather than physical ones. These illnesses are hard to treat with medication or even counseling. But ministry to the spirit of a person with the love of Christ is often very helpful in these situations.

The spiritual healing ministry is not intended to supplant those who have dedicated their lives to serving the health care needs of others. God can use doctors, nurses, psychiatrists, and other health care professionals just as much as he uses priests, sisters, and lay people whom he has blessed with gifts of healing prayer. Prayer often supplements the work of medical personnel by bringing peace, hope, and courage to the patient. Jesus continues his healing ministry by means of supernatural and natural healing processes and sometimes by a union of the two.

My experience with healing prayer has resulted in the development of a method that I find to be not only practical but pastorally responsible as well.

First of all, I approach the prayer with expectant faith. I know that God will hear and answer every prayer for healing. The fact that he may answer in a way that I don't expect doesn't affect my faith. I believe that he will act in power in response to my prayer. Before I pray I stir up my own faith with a silent prayer to the Holy Spirit, then I exhort the person or persons I am praying with to be open to receiving God's power. I remind them of the faith manifested by the lady with the hemorrhage whose healing is recorded in the New Testament. The lady reached out to touch his garment, believing that if she did so she would be healed. She knew that Jesus had the power to heal, and she believed that his power would heal her if she only approached him. This is the kind of faith that everyone should have. Jesus has the power, and if we get in touch with that power in faith Jesus will heal.

I then touch the person I am praying with. I realize that I have no power to heal but that I am only a channel of God's healing. A caring touch is a way to communicate God's love. Sometimes the caring touch is more significant for healing prayer than the words offered to God because it shows love. Often the person being prayed with senses something through touch—heat or a lessening of pain. These are indications of God's healing power at work. It is not inappropriate to ask the person being prayed with if such sensations are present. If they are, the prayer can be focused more clearly.

I have noticed that when I pray with others it is important to be joined by people who have gifts that I do not have. Many prayer groups and healing ministries have discovered that a group of several people ministering healing prayer can be more effective than just one individual. Healing is a body ministry and when several gifts are joined together to minister healing prayer, the effectiveness of the prayer is sometimes increased. I don't understand this mystery, but I have seen it work. God uses the mystical body of Christ to minister his healing.

The bottom line in all this is that people experience God, receive his love and peace, and are healed. Sometimes the healing is physical, sometimes it is spiritual or emotional, sometimes it is simply a strengthening to live the will of God in a fuller way.

The more I participate in healing prayer, the more I wonder whether those who experience God's strengthening for bearing with an illness and bearing fruit because of it are not really experiencing the greater healing.

Because of my experiences, I never hesitate to pray with people when I visit hospitals and other health care institutions. God has done things that have absolutely amazed me. I do, however, have a strong conviction that healing happens more consistently in the context of the sacraments. I am especially strong in my belief that the Eucharist puts us in such a special relationship with God that that is the time we should ask God for whatever we need. The Eucharist is the ultimate expression of God's love for us. It only makes sense to turn to him in prayer for healing after we have received him in the Eucharist.

My faith is stronger after I've received the Eucharist, both as a minister of healing and as a son asking God to heal me.

My personal experience with healing has actually

involved more inner healing than physical healing. My most vivid experience with inner healing was when I attended a retreat given by someone who has developed a method for inner healing. This man taught me how to come into God's love in order that God's love can produce healing in our lives.

More than three hundred times the Scriptures exhort us to "fear not, for I am with you." The priest exhorted me to relax in the reality of God's love the way that sunbathers lay on a beach soaking up the sun. "You don't have to try very hard at all," he said. "Just relax and soak up God's love. As you do, you'll become more whole inside."

I have experienced profound, deep, inner healing in my own life, and I know that God wants to do this for others. Inner healing is real and important. It involves utilizing some of the techniques of psychotherapy, but mostly it involves believing the words of God's love recorded in the Scriptures and absorbing the grace of the sacraments. The sacrament of Reconciliation especially has some specific graces to offer in this regard. The grace that forgives sin can also remove the scars of sin from our lives, even the sins of others that have produced scars in our own lives.

It is simply amazing for me to know that I can be a minister of God's love. And that is what healing is all about: any Christian who prays in faith can be a minister of God's love.

EIGHT

Jesus, Be Great in Me

IN THE PRECEDING CHAPTERS I have tried to share some of the insights God has blessed me with during my two-and-a-half decades of service as a priest and bishop. I have offered a few slogans that you may find helpful as you try to grow closer to the Lord and to serve him more fruitfully. Before I bring this book to a close, I would like to share a few more slogans with you. I think that you will find that the truths they represent will help you to fall even more in love with Jesus Christ the Lord.

The first is what I call the Peter Principle. The Gospels depict Peter as a very weak man. He was often thick-headed, slow to learn, slow to submit to Christ, cowardly at the end. Yet Jesus loved this weak man and saw in him a great leader for his church. Peter is one of my favorite saints for this very reason. The way that Christ dealt with him gives me hope, for I am also a weak man. By examining Peter's life I have seen that although we have a problem with weakness, God doesn't. He sends his grace into our lives to cut through our weakness and to enable us to accomplish what he has for us.

The Peter Principle is a slogan we can all draw hope and strength from: God doesn't have a problem with weakness—we do. When we recognize how profound this truth is, we can say with Paul: "when I am weak, Christ is strong in me."

A related slogan is this: Every problem is an opportunity.

In the course of daily life we encounter many problems. When they first present themselves, our problems often seem overwhelming. We react by getting angry, depressed—or both. When problems arise we need to exercise our faith, we need to turn to Jesus Christ our Lord and ask him for the wisdom and strength to turn the problem into an opportunity for growth.

Christians talk a lot about bearing fruit. This was a favorite expression of Jesus and is a very important concept. A true disciple of the Lord is known by the fruit he or she bears. Paul lists some of these fruits for us: "love, joy, peace, patient endurance, kindness, generosity, faith, mildness and chastity" (Gal 5:22-23). Sometimes we look at that list of virtues and we feel that we aren't bearing good fruit. Perhaps we've just exchanged harsh words with someone, or been selfish, or something similar.

Don't despair. Remember this slogan: There are pits in the fruits. Every good piece of fruit has a pit in the middle. To make the fruit edible you have to remove the pit. Our Christian lives work in similar ways. Until the day that Christ has made us perfect, we will always stumble a bit. When this happens we have to rely on his mercy and grace. We pick ourselves up, dust ourselves off, and continue. We remove the pit from the fruit and serve the fruit. Christ our Lord does this for us!

The last slogan I want to leave you with is one of the most profound truths I have ever heard: Jesus, be great in me.

This sentiment was first shared with me by an elderly priest who prayed those words each day before celebrating the Eucharistic liturgy. "Jesus, be great in me," he prayed.

The first time I heard him say that I thought, "How arrogant. A priest should be humble and should appear humble so that God can be seen as the great one."

But, fortunately, I didn't allow that rash judgment of my brother priest to remain with me. I reflected about his prayer, and as I did I began to realize how profoundly right and good this simple prayer is.

Jesus, be great in me. What that means is that the fruit of the Lord should be apparent in me. People who know me realize how weak I am, how thoughtless and selfish I can be. When they see me bearing good fruit—being loving, generous, forgiving—they will realize that that is Jesus acting through me. If I am truly humble—pointing to Jesus by the way I live my life—he will be seen as the great one.

As I have allowed this prayer to take root in my life, I have experienced a great deal of freedom. I no longer have to worry about what people think about me. As long as people are getting in touch with Jesus through me, I am bearing good fruit and I am free.

Jesus, be great in me. It's a great way to conclude a discussion of the Lordship of Jesus Christ. I hope you will make that your prayer. God bless you.

Other Books of Interest from Servant Books

Let the Fire Fall
Father Michael Scanlan, T.O.R.

The powerful personal story of Father Michael's dramatic encounter with the Holy Spirit. A modern-day adventure story with a very personal and direct message for the reader. $6.95

Straight from the Heart
A Call to the New Generation
Father John Bertolucci

A powerful and direct call to today's young people to choose a radical Christian life-style from today's foremost Catholic evangelist. $4.95

Rejoice in Me
A Pocket Guide to Daily Scriptural Prayer
Msgr. David E. Rosage

A reflection from the Psalms for each day of the year. An ideal size and format for the Christian on the go who wants to take time aside with God each day. $3.95

Available at your Christian bookstore or from
**Servant Publications • Dept. 209 • P.O. Box 7455
Ann Arbor, Michigan 48107**
Please include payment plus $.75 per book
for postage and handling
*Send for your FREE catalog of Christian
books, music, and cassettes.*